Beginner's Guide to Investing: How to Invest Like A Pro.

Table Of Contents

Introduction

I hope that this book on how to invest for beginners will give you a simple, easy-to-understand guide on how to invest.

This book is meant to be a simple step-by-step guide to how to invest for beginners. Learn how to invest for beginners by investing in stocks, bonds, and mutual funds. Investing can be an intimidating task for some people. I hope to help you learn how to invest for beginners and have a safe, secure future.

This book is written to help you learn how to invest for beginners. You will learn how to invest in stocks, bonds, and mutual funds. There are many investment opportunities out there. The goal of this book is to give you a simple, easy-to-understand guide on how to invest for beginners.

It is important that you carefully consider your investment goals before you begin investing. You must keep a record of your investments from day one and track your progress. This book will help you in that regard and give you some insights into a few different methods of investing.

I'm sure you've heard it before... "Wealth is in the eye of the beholder", or "Time is money". What does this mean? It means that, whatever your goal is, time will be needed to achieve it.

If you want to make a lot of money, you need to invest your time wisely. A wise man once said: "Money makes money... and success breeds success". This means that if you wish to make more money, you need to invest your time in wealth-building activities which will give birth to more money-making opportunities.

So how can you do this? By investing your time wisely. What are these wealth-building activities? That's exactly what we are going to learn here. Without further ado, let's get started with the basics of investing for beginners!

Chapter 1: Types of investments

You might have heard about investments, but don't know what to do with your hard-earned money. To invest your money, you need to know a little bit of information about the different types of investment.

There are several types of investments, and each investment has its pros and cons. You need to choose the right kind of investment that suits your needs.

In this chapter, we will learn about some of the popular investments available today.

Understand your options

The first thing you should do is to determine your risk tolerance. This is especially important if you are a beginner. You need to understand that investing can be risky and there are no guarantees of making money. This means that you must be willing to accept the risk of losing all the money you put in, but also accept the chance of making double or triple your initial investment.

If you are a beginner, then you should start with only a small percentage of your overall assets. This will allow the money to grow over time as it gets invested in more and more assets. You need to remember that it will also have some losses as well, but over time it should balance out.

You can have an easier time by investing in mutual funds which are professionally managed by fund managers or other investment professionals who have a history of outperforming comparable market indexes (or their benchmark). If they underperform, then they provide less return than if they had chosen the index fund or index as their benchmark.

If you are still uncomfortable with this process, then you can look at other alternatives such as Exchange Traded Funds (ETFs) and Exchange Traded Notes (ETNs). These investments provide greater diversification and lower costs than mutual funds.

These are just a few of the many investment options available to you. You should consider all the options and decide what is best for you. As a beginner, you should start with mutual funds or ETFs and slowly build up your portfolio over time.

Once you have made your decision, then there are some other things that you should think about when investing for beginners.

What is Risk Tolerance?

When we talk about risk tolerance, it is a measure of how much risk you are willing to take on. If you have more risk tolerance, then you will be willing to invest in different types of investments that have greater potential for bigger returns. But they also come with higher levels of risk.

If you have less risk tolerance, then you will try to limit the amount of risk that you take on. This means that you will need to invest in assets that are less risky and come with smaller potential returns. However, this also means that they are safer than other types of investments.

If we want to define the two terms, "risk" and "return," then both are related in many different ways. Let's look at the definitions for both terms and how they apply to invest:

Risk: The chance or possibility of loss or injury. Also referred to as volatility (the magnitude of the loss changes). This type is usually associated with investments because any investment has a chance of loss associated with it. The higher the expected return on an investment, the higher the level of risk as well.

Return: The profit or gain that is made on investment over time. It also refers to income that is received from an investment over time. If the investment is a good one, then you will see that it provides higher returns over time.

How do I determine my risk tolerance?

Here are a few questions that you can ask yourself to determine your risk tolerance:

Do you have a long time horizon?

If so, then you have more time to recover from losses. You can also look at the opportunity cost of holding on to your money for longer periods (i.e. what else could you do with the money in the meantime).

How much would I lose if I lost it all?

This is an important question because it allows you to determine how much loss you could accept before you would give up on investing altogether. If losing money will be too painful, then it is best to invest in less risky assets that will provide smaller returns over time. This allows you to reduce the amount of stress that comes with investing in high-risk assets.

What is your tolerance for stress?

This question is related to the previous one because it goes into further detail about what level of loss or pain would be acceptable for you. You should try and understand how much stress can be tolerated when investing in different types of assets.

For example, if we are talking about a stock market crash, then this type of event usually happens very slowly over time. If we are talking about an event like 9/11, then we are talking about a very sudden change in the market. How do you handle these types of events and how do they affect your stress level?

How much risk are you willing to take?

This is one of the most important questions. You should determine how much risk you are willing to take on. If you have a high appetite and tolerance for risk, then you should look at investing in different types of assets that offer higher potential returns over time.

Do you need to grow your money over time?

If you do not need to grow your money over time, then this is an important question because there are many different options available. However, if your goal is to save for retirement or other long-term goals, then there is more pressure on maximizing the returns that can be made from investments over time.

This also means that there will be more pressure on trying to find new investment opportunities that will generate higher returns over time.

How should I plan where to invest?

There are many different options available to you as a beginner. You should first decide what type of investments interest you the most and then research them more in-depth. Then you can try to determine if it makes sense to invest in those assets or not.

Firstly, you need to know what your goal is. Do you want to be able to retire at 40? Do you want to provide for your family? Are you starting a business and need capital?

Once you have identified your goal, then you can figure out how much capital you need and what the time frame is. If you need the money in a few years, then you can look at options like stocks and bonds. If you are looking to transfer wealth to your children, then there are other options also available.

You also need to figure out what your appetite for risk is. If you get butterflies in your stomach when the stock market moves down, then it may not be appropriate for you to invest in stocks. S&P 500 index funds have low volatility and are great for long-term investment if you have the risk tolerance for it.

Once you have figured out your goal and risk tolerance, then it is time to start researching where to invest. The best place to start is with an online brokerage account like TD Ameritrade or Fidelity Investments.

These brokers offer the most diverse set of investment options available anywhere on the planet today and will give back every penny that they make from commissions in more fees charged on mutual funds or ETFs that they have available.

Once you open up an account, ask for advice from a stockbroker or financial advisor who works there. They will be able to give advice based on what types of investments interest you and will help guide you through the process of opening up an account and getting started.

Which type of investments should I start with?

There is no right or wrong answer to this question. It is important to understand that different types of investments react differently to different economic conditions and trends.

A value investor will prefer a stock that has a low price relative to its earnings, while a momentum investor will prefer one that has been increasing in price the most recently.

A risk-averse investor will go for something like a bond fund while a risk-taker will go for something like an emerging market stock fund. The point is that you should know what risk level you are comfortable with and what kind of returns you expect.

Then you can start researching the options available to you and determine which makes the most sense for you specifically.

Now, we will cover some of the different types of investments and their pros and cons.

Stocks

Investing in stocks can be risky for beginners. But, it is the best way to make money over time. This chapter will give you some tips on how to invest in stocks for beginners.

What Stock Is:

Stock is a share of ownership in a company. When you buy a stock, you become an owner of that company. You are entitled to receive any profits that the company makes and also entitled to any dividends that the company decides to payout. If the company pays dividends, it is usually quarterly or annually, depending on what the board of directors decides. Some companies pay dividends more often than others.

Generally, companies with higher growth tend not to pay dividends as often or as much as stable companies with lower growth rates.

At some point in time, whether you sell your shares or not, you may be eligible for receiving cash payments when the company goes public again (i.e., after being acquired by someone else).

How To Invest In Stocks:

Now that you have a basic idea of what stock investing is all about, how do you go about investing? Well, there are many ways and each has its pros and cons:

Direct Stock Purchase

When you buy stock directly from a company, you are buying shares from the company itself. The company may sell to you directly or it may use an intermediary like a broker or a bank (i.e., buy-side).

If you are buying shares directly from the company, you will be creating your account with the company and all transactions will be done electronically. You can also do this with a broker, but there is typically a fee involved in doing so.

When you buy shares from a company directly, there are usually no fees involved if it is being done through their website or by phone. Brokers may charge fees for setting up an account and making purchases, but there are no commissions charged when you buy shares through them.

Your broker will charge a fee, typically around $10 to $20 per trade.

Buy-Side Stock Purchase

When you buy stock through a broker or a bank, you are buying shares from the intermediary (i.e., the buy-side).

The buy-side has an account with the company and buys shares on your behalf. The intermediary then transfers the shares to your name.

Brokers and banks typically charge fees for setting up an account as well as for buying or selling shares. These fees tend to be lower than when purchasing directly from the company because of the higher volume of transactions that they do.

Pros and Cons:

Buying a stock is not risk-free. You can lose money if the company did not do well and went bankrupt or the price of the stock went down to zero. Some other risks are specific to stocks.

The Pros:

Owning a stock means that you own part of a business. Therefore, you generally have a vested interest in seeing the company succeed. If it does well, then you will reap some of the rewards as well. When you buy a stock, you generally want to hold it for some time until there is an attractive exit strategy such as selling it at an increased price (i.e., profit). Therefore, you have to look at your investment from a longer-term perspective rather than worrying about what happens on any given day or week, or month.

When investing in stocks, you don't need much money to start with because most brokerage firms allow investors to buy fractional shares - where you can buy less than one share at a time (e.g., 0.5 shares). You can also choose how much money each month that you want to invest in stocks and purchase more when your monthly amount gets used up (i.e., by using dollar-cost averaging).

The Cons:

As an owner of a stock, you can only profit if the company does well. If a company does poorly, then you will also lose money. Stocks are very volatile and can have a high degree of risk, especially if you don't have much experience investing in stocks. Therefore, it is best to start investing in stocks when market conditions are favorable (i.e., when the market is rising or flat) and not during a bear market (i.e., declining markets).

Types of Stocks:

There are many types of stocks that you can buy but generally, they are broken down into three categories - growth stocks, value stocks, and income stocks (also called dividends):

Growth Stocks:

These are companies that are growing very quickly and thus have higher risks associated with them because there is greater uncertainty with these companies than with value or income stocks.

Because of the greater risk associated with growth stocks, they tend to return more money than value or income stocks over time as well as having higher returns on average than other types of stock like bonds or cash (e.g., money market accounts). This makes them a good choice for someone who has longer time horizons (i.e., > 5 years).

Value Stocks:

Also called "blue-chip stocks," these are companies that are usually very stable and have a history of paying dividends. They usually have lower growth rates than growth stocks but they typically pay dividends more often. Therefore, they tend to be better choices for someone with shorter time horizons (e.g., 1-3 years).

Income Stocks:

These are companies that are growing slower than both value and growth stocks but tend to pay dividends more often than value stocks do. These companies also tend to have higher yields than either value or growth stocks.

The companies that fall into this category would generally be the safest type of stock and would be a good choice for someone who has longer time horizons (i.e., > 5 years) but still wants some income from their investments periodically while still taking significant risks with their investments over the long term (i.e., > 5 years).

Bonds

Bonds are debt instruments created by companies, municipalities, and government agencies. Bonds are generally a good investment alternative for investors with a long-term horizon.

Bonds are created when a company or government wants to raise funds to finance large projects. Bonds can be issued as fixed income securities or floating rate securities. The fixed income part of the bond means that the company will pay back the bondholder at a certain date with interest. Floating rate bonds are bonds that change interest rates based on an index. When interest rates rise, these changes will appear in the floating rate bonds. These types of bonds are generally viewed as riskier than fixed-income bonds because the interest rate could change at any time. Fixed income securities have more stability, but also offer lower returns than bonds with floating rates.

There are different types of companies and different levels of governments that issue bonds to investors. Companies can issue corporate or municipal bonds while governments can issue Treasuries, Municipal Securities, or Government National Mortgage Association (Ginnie Mae) securities. Government Securities have different levels of risk depending on the type of security and level of government it was issued from. However, all government securities are viewed as low risk/low reward investments because even if they lose value they will not default on their obligations.

Investors buy bonds from companies and governments because they want to receive a return on their investment. Investors can buy bonds for the following reasons:

Getting Income: When investors purchase bonds, they will receive a certain amount of interest payments throughout the term of the bond. This is called income. Getting Value: Bonds are used by investors to achieve value in two ways: capital appreciation and price stability. Capital appreciation refers to the increase in the value of the bond when interest rates fall. Price stability refers to investors who purchase bonds based on their need for a stable investment that will not change rapidly in price over time. Speculation and Trading: Bonds are also used by investors as speculative tools that can be sold when necessary or traded for other products that have more potential for growth.

Bonds have different types of maturity dates, which represent the time when the company or government will pay back the investor with interest payments. The maturity date is determined by how long an investor wants to hold onto a bond before selling it again on the market or redeeming it for its full value from the issuer. The maturity date can range from one month to 30 years depending on how long an investor wants to hold onto a specific bond.

The type of bond that an investor purchase is determined by the level of risk they want to take on in their investment portfolio. There are different types of bonds: municipal bonds, corporate bonds, and government securities. Municipal bonds are issued by local governments, municipal authorities, or a state. Corporate bonds are issued by corporations that do business worldwide. Government securities can be issued by the United States government, states or municipalities. Treasuries are the most secure and lowest interest rate option while Ginnie Mae securities are viewed as riskier because they are issued against real estate loans.

Bonds can be purchased based on their coupon yield, which is determined by the interest rate paid to the investor for holding onto the bond for a specified period. The coupon yield is expressed as an annualized percentage rate (APR). In this case, investors will receive an annualized return based on holding onto a specific bond for a year before selling it again on the market. Bonds can also be purchased based on their price; however, this method may result in greater losses when purchasing higher-yielding bonds because higher yields generally mean greater risk for investors in terms of losses when interest rates drop and prices fall.

Bonds can be purchased through brokers, banks, mutual funds, money market funds, or other financial institutions. The cost of a bond is determined by the price that the investor pays for the bond and the interest rate that they receive from it.

Investors can purchase bonds directly from an issuer through websites or over the phone. Investors can also purchase bonds through a broker or other financial institution. This method is referred to as indirect purchasing because investors are buying a security that has already been purchased from another source. This is generally viewed as more expensive for investors because they will be charged additional fees by their broker or financial institution.

If an investor wants to sell their bonds before they mature, they can do so through a broker or directly through the company that issued their bond. The price of bonds can also change depending on how many people want to buy and sell them on the market at any given time.

Pros and Cons:

The Pros:

Bonds are generally a good investment for investors with a long-term horizon. Investors who purchase bonds will be able to receive gain on their investment from the coupon yield that they will receive throughout the term of the bond. Also, if investors sell their bonds before they mature, they will be able to sell their bonds at market prices and may be able to sell them at a significant gain depending on how many people are buying and selling them on the market. If an investor holds onto their bond until maturity, they can redeem them for full value from the issuer.

The Cons:

Investors who purchase bonds based on maturity dates may not receive a market price if they decide to sell them during periods of high-interest rates or when interest rates fall. The interest rate and price of bonds may also change over time due to changes in global economic conditions or political situations. Bonds also have less potential for growth than stocks because companies issuing bonds generally have less growth potential than other stocks included in an investor's portfolio. Bond prices are also more stable than stock prices; however, this is not always viewed as a positive factor because many investors want to invest in products that have more potential for growth rather than stability over time.

Indexes

A stock market is a volatile place and there are millions of people who are trying to find the best way to make money in it, but many of them get lost in the search for the best investment.

Indexes are the staple of the financial world. They are used by every mutual fund in the world to represent a particular sector or type of stock. They are used as benchmarks to compare the performance of individual stocks and mutual funds against. In fact, most people don't even know why they use indexes, they just do it because everyone else does it.

The first thing an investor should know is that indexes are not usually traded on a regular stock exchange. They have their many investors are seeking market value when you purchase them on an exchange, but that's not what I'm referring to here. In speaking about indexes, I'm referring to how they are used as a benchmark for an individual stock's performance. The price for which you can purchase shares in indexes is determined by supply and demand and tends to stay fairly close to whatever it was when you purchased your shares (although there can be minor fluctuations). This is unlike individual stocks which tend to go up and down in value from day to day depending upon supply and demand (and other factors).

In other words, the price of indexes will remain relatively stable if there is no major change in their underlying holdings. Conversely, changes in underlying holdings or technical factors can cause a company's share price to fluctuate.

So, if you want to invest in an index fund that tracks the performance of the Dow Jones Industrial Average, you don't have to worry about day-to-day fluctuations. You just have to know that your investment will fluctuate as the underlying stocks do.

Indexes are one of the best ways to start with investing in stocks.

Stock markets are made up of indexes, which mean they are a representation of how a specific real-world asset or group of assets is performing. So if you want to invest in Indexes, you will be investing in a specific group of companies with your assets.

An index is defined as an average or representative value that can be used as a benchmark for comparison purposes or to serve as a standard for measurement. So it is an industry average that allows us to track how well it is performing. It allows investors to see how well their investments are performing when compared against other indexes throughout the country or world.

Types of Indexes:

Market Capitalization (Total Market Value) Indexes

This is the most common type of index. To find the total market valuation, you simply add up the number of shares outstanding and multiply it by the market price per share. The major indexes such as the Dow Jones Industrial Average, S&P 500, and Nasdaq Composite are examples of market-capitalization-weighted indexes.

Price-Weighted Indexes

These are different from the market capitalization-weighted indexes because they are based on stock price instead of the total number of shares outstanding. If a company has a high stock price, it will have an impact on their weight in this type of index regardless if there is a small or large number of shares outstanding. The result is that companies with higher stock prices have more influence in a price-weighted index than companies with lower stock prices or fewer shares outstanding.

Inverse Indexes

These are also called bearish indexes because they tend to rise when the underlying market declines and vice-versa; therefore there is an inverse relationship between these two types of indexes i.e., when one rises, the other falls and vice versa; this can be confusing as both indexes are usually calculated with the same components.

The Dow Jones Industrial Average is a price-weighted index because it is made up of 30 stocks and the price of each stock is multiplied by its respective number of shares outstanding. The S&P 500, on the other hand, is a market capitalization-weighted index; the S&P 500 Index contains 500 stocks that are weighted based on their total market value.

Some stock indexes are weighted based on both market capitalization and price; these indexes are normally referred to as "capitalization-weighted."

Pros and Cons:

The Pros:

1) Indexes are easy and inexpensive to buy and sell. The price you pay for them usually remains fairly close to what it was when you purchased the shares. Also, buying and selling them is quick and easy. You can sell them or buy more of them whenever you want. Contrast this with individual stocks which can be difficult to sell at times (if there isn't much demand for it) because they can change in value from day-to-day (depending upon supply and demand).

2) Indexes provide a low-cost way for beginning investors to get started in investing by spreading their risk across many different companies or sectors at once. This type of diversification is generally considered a good strategy for people who are just starting out in investing since they don't know enough about individual companies yet (they could be high risk). A mutual fund takes care of all the management decisions, such as when to buy and sell, and provides the investor with a single investment that represents a large group of stocks.

3) Indexes offer greater stability (less fluctuation) than individual stocks.

4) Indexes represent high-volume investments because there are many investors seeking to purchase them (and/or many investors seeking to sell them). This means that they tend to be very liquid (easily bought and sold). In other words, you can easily get in or get out of an index when you want. Contrast that with individual stocks which can be difficult to sell, even if there is a lot of demand for them (which means you need to have a plan for how you'll get out if the stock price isn't where you want it).

5) Indexes have low operating costs because they do not require portfolio managers or analysts. They also provide investors with instant diversification across many different companies in a sector at virtually no extra cost. That's why mutual funds often use indexes as their benchmarks for performance.

6) Investing in indexes doesn't require any special skills on the part of the investor. You don't need vision or ability to pick winning stocks - just patience because sometimes it takes years before you see a profit.

The Cons:

1) Indexes do not represent the best investments. They represent average ones. This means they are often at a disadvantage to individual stocks and mutual funds that are managed by skilled professionals who are constantly looking for ways to beat the market. Indexes also represent underlying companies that have gone through a lot of changes over time, which may not be reflected in their current prices. For example, your index might include companies whose owners have already sold their shares, leaving them with new owners who might not be as capable as the original owners (who might have been more concerned about the long-term prospects of the company).

2) Since many investors use indexes as benchmarks for performance, it can be difficult to sell an individual stock if you're not satisfied with its performance because it might drag down your overall index performance. Therefore, you may keep a stock in your portfolio longer than you should just because it's part of an index - even if it's performing poorly. Contrast this with individual stocks where you can sell them at any time because there isn't any benchmark for their performance to drag down your overall results.

3) In addition to being relatively stable, indexes tend to provide low returns. As I said, they represent average companies, which means they don't perform as well as the best companies. This is why you see mutual funds that invest in indexes have low returns. They're getting the same results you will get.

4) Indexes are more likely to be sold if there is a large-scale change in their underlying holdings. For example, if a company you own starts a new war or gets sued for something (which might cause their share price to drop), your index might sell your stock to avoid any further damage to its overall performance.

5) Indexes are not necessarily safe investments because some of their underlying assets can become unreliable or unprofitable (due to changes in technology or other factors). This happens frequently with stocks and commodities because new uses for them are being developed all the time - sometimes leaving them behind obsolete.

6) It takes longer for an index investor to make money than it does an individual stock or mutual fund investor because they aren't as skilled at picking winners. It's hard to predict which stocks are going to go up and which ones will go down, but sooner or later you'll be able to tell the difference between a good stock and a bad one.

Options

Options are the most widely traded derivative in the world. They are also one of the most complex financial instruments. Options allow investors to speculate or hedge their positions, depending on whether you're buying or selling an option. Because options involve the future price of a stock, they have a much greater risk than traditional securities trading.

If you have ever spent time in Las Vegas, you know that, when you walk in, there are many kinds of games to choose from. Some of them seem quite simple: they just take your money and give you nothing in return. Others are quite complex.

Options are a bit like that. You can use them to speculate on stocks or to protect yourself against stock price swings, which is known as hedging. The complexity arises from the fact that options do not pay out cash by themselves, they merely give the holder the right (but not the obligation) to buy or sell a stock at a specified price by a specified date in exchange for a small payment called the option premium.

Types of Options:

There are two main types of options, Call and Put. A call option gives the holder the right to buy at a certain price at a specific time. A put option gives the holder the right to sell at a certain price at a specific time.

The difference between buying and selling an option is that if you buy an option, you have two choices: either you can exercise your right to buy or sell at a specified price, or allow it to expire without taking action (known as letting it expire worthlessly).

If you sell an option, on the other hand, there are two possible outcomes:
1. You can reap all profits before expiration;
2. You will lose money if your client exercises his/her options before expiration (unless he/she pays for this privilege).

How do they work?

Let's say you think Apple stock is going to go up over the next month. You could buy Apple stock outright, but you're worried about what will happen if it doesn't go up as much as you expect.

Instead of buying Apple stock, you could decide to buy an option on it instead. An option on Apple stock gives you rights to over 100 shares of Apple stock (either buying or selling rights). Let's say that one contract costs $3 (see below for an explanation of what this means).

n that case, you would have paid $300 for the option, which can now be sold on to someone else. If Apple stock goes up to $250, then you can exercise your right to buy it at $200. But if Apple stock falls to $150, you are happy that you only paid $300 for the option, since it was never a good deal at $200.

The great thing about options is that they give you leverage. This means you only have to put up a small amount of money to control 100 shares of Apple stock. If Apple falls in price, then your loss would also be small (assuming you bought the option for less than it is worth). On the other hand, if Apple goes up in price then you will make a nice profit on your investment.

Let's look at an example:

You think that Twitter Inc (TWTR) is going to go up in price over the next month or so. It's currently trading at $35 per share and it has a 52-week high price of $40 per share. You decide that you want to buy some Twitter stock but don't want to commit a large sum of money upfront because there is still some downside risk (meaning that TWTR could fall in value). So you decide to buy an option instead. You happen to find a buyer who is willing to sell you an option for $2 per contract. There are 100 shares per contract, so you have just paid $200 for the option ($2 x 100 x 1000 = 200).

Your cost of entry into this trade is now only 200, while your upside potential is unlimited (since TWTR could go up in price by any amount). The maximum loss that you could incur would be $200 if TWTR fell to its 52 week low of $20 per share. If TWTR falls in price, then your loss is limited to the amount that you invested in the option. If TWTR doubles in price then your profit would also double and be worth twice as much as it was before (assuming you bought this option for less than it was worth).

The options market is very fast-moving and can be quite expensive once all commissions are included. That's why many investors choose to buy options on the exchange-traded funds (ETF)s like the SPDR S&P 500 ETF (SPY) or the Emerging Markets ETF (EEM). When buying options on an ETF, it's important to understand that they are not the same as buying the actual stocks within the ETF. For example, while you have unlimited upside potential when buying an option on an ETF, you don't have unlimited downside potential. In other words, your loss is limited to the amount that you paid for the option.

These options are often referred to as "options on a basket". Another advantage of buying options on a basket is that they can be used with less capital than buying each of those stocks individually. If you are going to buy options, then it's best to understand exactly what you're paying for by looking at the option premium per contract and how many contacts are in each contract (or put another way: how much stock is in each contract).

The Pros and Cons:

The Pros:

Options are not directly correlated to the stock market. This means that even if the market goes down, you can still make a profit.

The Options Market is liquid and has many participants, so there is plenty of liquidity.

Because options have time value, they can be used for speculation or hedging.

The Cons:

Options are risky because you have to pay a premium.

You can lose money even if the stock goes up. This is especially true if you buy "out of the money" options.

Like most financial instruments, options have a time value: the further out you go, the more risk there is that the market could move against you and wipe out your position. The farther out in time you go, the greater your exposure to potential losses. Besides, option premiums are subject to change as market conditions change and as volatility increases or decreases.

Commodity Futures

Commodity Futures is a form of trading that allows the investor to speculate on future commodity prices. Some traders have used this technique to make a fortune. However, some have lost everything they invested.

A futures contract is an agreement between two parties that have been made for future delivery of a particular commodity at a predetermined price. The contract is negotiated and agreed upon today but will not be settled until sometime in the future.

Before we look at the steps involved in Commodities Futures Trading, let us look at the various kinds of commodities that are traded using this technique.

Types of Commodities:

Agricultural Commodities:

The main ones are wheat, rice, corn, and sugar. Energy Commodities: Oil and other energy sources such as natural gas, coal, and uranium.

Precious Metals:

Gold and silver are included in this category along with platinum and palladium.

Industrial Metals:

Iron ore, copper, lead, and zinc are some examples of industrial metals that fall under this category.

Livestock:

Live cattle are an example of livestock that can be traded using commodity futures contracts.

Currency:

This group consists of currency forwards (or foreign exchange), options on currencies as well as index futures.

How Commodity Futures Trading Works:

The investor can either buy or sell a futures contract. If the investor is bullish on the commodity or expects its price to rise, then he/she will buy. The investor can also sell a futures contract if he/she expects the commodity's price to fall.

As long as the contract is open, then the buyer and seller are obliged to fulfill their obligations under the contract. The buyer has to take delivery of the commodity from the seller and pay him/her the agreed-upon price. The seller has to accept the delivery of commodities from the buyer and pay him/her accordingly.

A futures contract is also referred to as an option on a commodity because it allows you to buy or sell a particular commodity at an agreed-upon fee (i.e., strike price) at some future date in time (the expiry date).

For example, you might be able to purchase an option that gives you rights for delivery of 100 barrels of crude oil next month at a predetermined price. However, before your option expires, you have an opportunity to sell your option for a profit if it has increased in value since your original purchase.

You may also be able to sell your option for a profit before it expires if you believe that the market value of the commodity is going to fall.

An option has two main characteristics:

The buyer has the right but not the obligation to buy or sell an asset at a set price on or before a specified date. The seller must fulfill delivery of an asset at a fixed price on or before a specified date.

There are two kinds of options that can be purchased - call options and put options. Call options give you the right to buy and put options give you the right to sell.

For example, you might purchase a call option from someone who owns some barrels of oil which he/she is willing to sell at an agreed-upon price in six months. If he/she sells you this option, then he/she will be required to honor this agreement (i.e., deliver 100 barrels of oil) and pay you for it when it expires (i.e., six months later).

On the other hand, if he/she gives you this option and you do not use it, then nothing happens and no money changes hands between the two parties involved in this transaction. The person who buys an option is referred to as the holder of the option. The person who sells an option is referred to as the writer of the option.

Buying a Call Option:

A call option gives you the right to buy a particular commodity for a predetermined price at some point in time in the future. For example, you might purchase a call option that allows you to buy 100 barrels of crude oil at $75/barrel in three months.

This means that if you do decide to use this option, then you will have to pay $75 for each barrel of crude oil that you buy from the seller. However, if you do not use this option and do not purchase any barrels of oil then nothing happens and no money changes hands between the two parties involved in this transaction.

In other words, there is no obligation on your part to purchase any barrels of oil from the seller even though he/she has agreed to sell it at $75/barrel.

If you did decide to use your call option for 100 barrels of crude oil at $75/barrel, then delivery will be made by taking possession of 100 barrels of crude oil from some company (i.e., an exchange). The company will have purchased these barrels for $75/barrel from the seller. He/she will then deliver the 100 barrels to you at $75/barrel. In return for this, you will pay him/her $75 x 100 = $7,500.

You can also buy one call option for several barrels of oil at the same time. Let's say that you purchased a call option for 100 barrels of oil at $75/barrel in three months. In addition to this, you also purchased a call option for 50 barrels of oil at the same price but delivered in six months.

This is known as a "calendar spread". So, if you purchase two or more call options (i.e., buy two or more call options simultaneously), then these are known as "vertical spreads". The difference between purchasing just one option and purchasing two or more options simultaneously is that your risk is spread across two or more different delivery dates and not just one single date.

This means that each of your options has an expiration date - one in three months and the other in six months. On each of these dates, you have an opportunity to sell your option(s) for a profit if they have increased in value since your original purchase.

A call option is also referred to as an "insurance policy" because it gives you the right to buy a commodity at a predetermined price if you want to but you can also get rid of this right before it expires. So, if the price of the commodity rises above the strike price - i.e., above $75/barrel - then you will have made a profit on your option (i.e., insurance policy).

On the other hand, if the price of the commodity falls below the strike price - i.e., below $75/barrel - then your option will expire worthlessly and no money will change hands between the two parties involved in this transaction. In other words, your "insurance policy" would be worthless and would not protect you against any losses on this particular transaction.

Buying a Put Option:

A put option gives you the right to sell (i.e., deliver) a particular commodity for a predetermined price at some point in time in the future. If you do decide to use this option, then you will have to deliver 100 barrels of crude oil at $75 each within three months (the delivery date).

However, if you do not use this option and do not deliver 100 barrels of oil, then nothing happens and no money changes hands between the two parties involved in this transaction. In other words, there is no obligation on your part to make any deliveries to the seller even though he/she has agreed to buy it at $75/barrel.

If you did decide to use your put option for 100 barrels of crude oil at $75/barrel, then delivery will be made by taking possession of 100 barrels of crude oil from some company (i.e., an exchange).

The company will have bought these barrels for $75/barrel from the seller. He/she will then deliver the 100 barrels to you at $75/barrel. In return for this, he/she will receive $75 x 100 = $7,500 from you.

You can also buy one put option for several barrels of oil at the same time. Let's say that you purchased a put option for 50 barrels of oil at $75/barrel in three months and another put option for 50 barrels of oil at the same price but delivery in six months. This is known as a "calendar spread".

So, if you purchase two or more call options (i.e., buy two or more put options simultaneously), then these are known as "vertical spreads". The difference between purchasing just one option and purchasing two or more options simultaneously is that your risk is spread across two or more different delivery dates and not just one single date.

This means that each of your options has an expiration date - one in three months and the other in six months. On each of these dates, you have an opportunity to sell your option(s) for a profit if they have increased in value since your original purchase.

A put option is also referred to as an "insurance policy" because it gives you the right to sell a commodity at a predetermined price if you want to but you can also get rid of this right before it expires.

So, if the price of the commodity rises above the strike price - i.e., above $75/barrel - then you will have made a profit on your option (i.e., insurance policy).

On the other hand, if the price of the commodity falls below the strike price - i.e., below $75/barrel - then your option will expire worthlessly and no money will change hands between the two parties involved in this transaction. In other words, your "insurance policy" would be worthless and would not protect you against any losses on this particular transaction.

You can also purchase a call option together with a put option at the same time. This is known as a "straddle" or "strangle".

For example, let's say that you purchase a put option for 100 barrels of oil at $75/barrel in three months and a call option for 100 barrels of oil at the same price but delivery in six months. This is known as a "calendar spread".

So, if you buy two or more call options (i.e., buy two or more put options simultaneously), then these are known as "vertical spreads". The difference between purchasing just one option and purchasing two or more options simultaneously is that your risk is spread across two or more different delivery dates and not just one single date.

This means that each of your options has an expiration date - one in three months and the other in six months. On each of these dates, you have an opportunity to sell your option(s) for a profit if they have increased in value since your original purchase.

The Pros and Cons:

The Pros:

Commodities are an important part of our daily lives. They are also things that we use in large quantities. This creates a scenario where the individual can accumulate a lot of wealth by simply investing in these commodities. This is the reason why commodity futures is considered to be one of the safest options for investments.

Another advantage of this technique is that it helps to minimize your losses as well as maximize your gains. This is because you can buy and sell your contract at the market price and set a stop price for when you wish to exit from a particular contract.

The Cons:

Peak hours are usually considered quite volatile and this can prove to be risky if you do not know much about it. The fact that it is traded on an exchange, means that it will always have some sort of volatility attached to it. However, if you want to make money from it, then you cannot be afraid of volatility as it plays an important role in profiting from this type of investment.

Cryptocurrency

Ever since the internet came about, technology has grown to be an integral part of our lives. This includes banking and asset management as well. With the advance of technology, we have seen the rise of cryptocurrency and blockchain technology. Cryptocurrency is a digital or virtual currency that uses cryptography for security. No central authority has control over it and it's not subject to regulation by any government or bank.

Cryptocurrency is open-source so no one owns or controls any cryptocurrency, in particular, thereby making it decentralized. It's exchanged between peers without an intermediary like a bank, company, or government. Cryptocurrencies get generated through mining which is solving complex mathematical problems using computers with high-end graphics cards running at a very high speed. Mining isn't as difficult anymore because each block on the blockchain contains a special hash that acts as a fingerprint for that block of transactions. The moment someone solves that hash and finds an answer that generates say 25 bitcoins, they can then send those bitcoins to their wallet and anyone looking at the blockchain can see that 25 new bitcoins were created.

The first cryptocurrency ever created was called Bitcoin in 2009 with its first transaction being made by Satoshi Nakamoto who is still anonymous to this day. Since then, there have been many other cryptocurrencies created like Ethereum, Ripple, Litecoin, and more. Their value is determined by how much people are willing to pay for them.

Many cryptocurrencies differ in design and purpose. Each cryptocurrency has a price, market cap, and unique features like anonymity, speed, etc.

Cryptocurrencies are just like stocks. They have a price that can increase or decrease based on various factors. The main difference between cryptocurrencies and stocks is that cryptocurrencies are decentralized and not associated with any particular government or company, they're open-source and used for anonymous transactions.

Cryptocurrencies can be traded on exchanges just like stock markets where people can buy and sell cryptocurrencies to make profits or losses depending on the price movement of the currency. The most popular exchanges are Binance, Coinbase, Poloniex, Kraken, Bitfinex, etc. There's also cloud mining where you can buy mining contracts from companies to mine the cryptocurrency for you instead of doing it yourself using your hardware. Cloud mining is great for those who don't have access to special hardware required for mining or those who cannot afford it due to the initial investment costs involved in purchasing these devices.

How to trade cryptocurrencies?

The best way to trade cryptocurrencies is by using exchanges. Exchanges are websites where you can buy and sell cryptocurrencies for another currency or fiat money (USD, EUR, GBP, etc.). Cryptocurrencies can be exchanged for other cryptocurrencies as well. Exchanges are run by companies who create an account and deposit their currency into it. When they deposit money into their account, they can trade them for cryptocurrencies like Bitcoin, Ethereum, etc. The transactions are done using the application programming interface (API). An application programming interface is a software that allows the exchange to interact with other applications and networks by sending requests over the internet. This API receives requests from a user who wants to buy a certain amount of say Bitcoin from yet another user who wants to sell it. The transaction gets verified and once payment has been made, it will be reflected in your wallet's balance in the exchange's database.

Mobile applications like Coinbase on Android or iOS allow users to buy and sell cryptocurrencies directly from their smartphone without even logging into the website itself.

How to store cryptocurrency?

Cryptocurrencies can be stored in an online or offline wallet. Online wallets are operated by companies and are very easy to use but they're vulnerable to hacks since they're connected to the internet. Offline wallets are the safest with no connectivity to the internet but require you to download the full blockchain which is a record of every transaction ever made on that currency's network. This takes a very long time and requires lots of storage space for each currency. Popular online wallets include Blockchain and Coinbase while popular offline wallets include Exodus, Jaxx, Electrum, etc.

Cryptocurrency Wallets:

There are two types of cryptocurrency wallets - a software wallet (desktop) or a hardware wallet (mobile). Software wallets are easier to use but hardware wallets are more secure. The software wallets require you to download their application from the company's website (usually a zip file) and then extract the files into a folder on your computer. They can only run on Windows, macOS, or Linux.

Hardware wallets are much easier to set up and use since all you have to do is plug them into your computer via USB and they'll auto-run the software for you. No downloading or installation required. Hardware wallets come with an integrated display that allows you to view transactions and balances, send & receive payments, etc. They also allow you to quickly connect to the internet using Wi-Fi or cellular data even if your computer is locked with a password or encryption key.

Popular hardware wallets include Trezor and Ledger Nano S. You can purchase these devices from their website directly where they ship internationally as well. Popular software wallets include Exodus, Electrum, Jaxx, etc which are available for free on Windows, macOS, and Linux operating systems but not mobile devices yet (except Jaxx).

The Pros and Cons:

The Pros:

1. Completely anonymous

2. Can be used to purchase goods and services

3. It's decentralized so no central authority or company is controlling it.

4. No government can control it or regulate it because cryptocurrency isn't recognized as a legal tender by any government in the world

5. You can have full control over your money and the transactions you make with it since cryptocurrency is stored in a digital wallet that only you own. From here, you can send and receive cryptocurrencies with anyone else who has a digital wallet.

The Cons:

1. The value of cryptocurrency is completely determined by its demand, meaning it's entirely dependent upon how popular it is since its value is directly tied to this. It's not connected with any physical assets like gold or silver or any currency controlled by a government. It's completely dependent upon the market which can fluctuate based on popularity and demand.

2. There are no safeguards from cyber-attacks and hacks so you could lose your money if your wallet is hacked or if someone steals your private key, making cryptocurrency extremely risky in that sense

Chapter 2: What are the best investments for beginners?

This chapter will provide you with tips on how to start investing in the stock market and beyond. It will also provide you with some very good investment strategies that you can use to get started in your first investment.

The first step is to decide on how you would like to invest. You need to decide whether you want to invest in stocks, bonds, or mutual funds. Each of these investments has advantages and disadvantages. The right choice is going to depend on your situation. It is also going to depend on your financial goals and what you are looking for in an investment.

The first step is important

The first step is to determine your goals. This will be your guiding light when you consider investments. You need to decide on whether you want to invest for income or growth. If you are looking for income, then you are better off with bonds or dividend stocks. Mutual funds are also a good choice. If you are looking for growth, then you are going to want to invest in blue-chip stocks (large, stable companies that offer good payouts) or mid-cap stocks (medium-sized companies).

If your goal is to use your investment for retirement and the money is not needed right away, then it would probably be best to invest in low-risk investments such as bond funds or dividend stocks instead of high-risk investments like blue-chip stocks. The lower-risk investments will provide more dependable returns and will probably be less risky than trying to time the market correctly when investing in blue-chip stocks.

If you are looking for something more exciting, then you are probably going to want to invest in alternative investments. These include hedge funds, real estate, oil and gas, timber, and gold. These investments can provide really good returns, but they are also very risky. They could come crashing down at any time. You should only consider alternative investments if you have a high-risk tolerance or if you intend to use the investment for short-term goals like buying a new car in two years or taking that dream vacation next summer.

There is one more thing that you need to consider when deciding what to invest in: how much money do you have and how much money does it make sense for you to put into each type of investment? This is an important question because it will determine what kind of strategies that you should employ with different types of investments.

Where should I invest my money?

This is a question that is often asked by new investors. It is also one that I am frequently asked about. The answer to this question often depends on what you are looking for in an investment.

An investor that wants to invest for the long term will often choose to invest in mutual funds, stocks, and bonds. These three investment options can provide you with a good rate of return over the long term. If you are looking for something that will give you your money back quickly, then you should look at putting your money in stocks and bonds.

You need to be careful if you decide to invest in stocks or bonds because they both fluctuate greatly in value. You also need to be careful not to invest too much of your net worth into one investment option or another because it can be difficult if not impossible to diversify your portfolio if you have all your wealth tied up in one place or another. I would recommend investing no more than 30% of your net worth in any one investment option when starting out investing for the first time. This will help ensure that you are diversified and spread the risk out over multiple different investments so you don't put all of your eggs into one basket or another.

For example, if you had $10,000 in the bank and a mutual fund that was expected to earn you a 10% rate of return, your investment options would be as follows:

$10,000 x 10% = $1,000. You could invest the full $10,000 into the mutual fund or you could split it up into different investment options. If you were to invest only 30% of your net worth into an investment option then you would have the following options:

$3,333.33 worth of stocks or bonds

$6,666.67 worth of mutual funds (assuming a 10% rate of return)

This is just one example but it gives you an idea about how to get started if you are interested in investing for the first time. This is often called diversification. Diversification is very important when it comes to investing because it will help offset some of the risks associated with investing in individual stocks and/or bonds. I like to think of diversification as being similar to spreading out your net worth over many different investments so that if one investment loses money then there will be others that will help offset any losses that may occur. Diversification also allows you to spread out your money over multiple different investments so that you can take advantage of the strengths of each investment option.

You should never put all your eggs into one basket. This is a mistake that many new investors make when they first start investing because they do not understand how to invest in the stock market and beyond.

How much should I have in stocks?

One of the most common questions that beginners ask, is how much money should I invest in stocks. The answer to this question depends on your financial situation and what your goals are.

The general rule is that you would like to have about 50% of your portfolio in stocks and 50% in bonds or cash equivalents. You should adjust this as you get older, as you get closer to retirement.

There are two main reasons why you would want to have a good portion of your portfolio invested in stocks. The first reason is that they have a better return on investment compared to bonds and cash equivalents. The second reason is that they can get hit with some market volatility that will decrease the value of your investments, but it also means that they have a better chance to increase the value of your investments over time as well. This makes them a good investment option for long-term goals such as retirement or college savings for children.

For example, if you were saving for college for your child, then you would not want to put all of your money in stocks. You would want to have some in cash equivalents or bonds. This will help protect you from market volatility.

Are mutual funds a good investment for beginners?

For most beginners, mutual funds are a good way to get started. A mutual fund is a personal investment that allows you to invest with a handful of other people to increase your profit potential. If the stock market goes up, your mutual fund will make more money for you.

If the stock market goes down, your mutual fund will lose less money than you would have lost if you had invested in an individual company yourself. Mutual funds provide a way that is relatively risk-free for you to get started investing.

Mutual funds are also good because they are easy to invest in. Once you buy one, you can set it and forget it. You don't have to continually monitor the performance of the stock market or your mutual fund. You can simply invest and forget about it until you want to sell the mutual fund.

How do I invest in a mutual fund:

The easiest way to invest in a mutual fund is to go through your bank or another source that offers them. Many banks provide access to various mutual funds for their customers as a way for them to manage their money better.

If you do not have access to a bank that offers mutual funds, you can purchase them through online brokerage firms such as E*Trade (http://www.etrade.com)or Charles Schwab (http://www.schwab.com). Both of these sites allow you to buy and sell individual stocks or mutual funds directly from your computer screen at any time of the day or night.

There are also mutual funds that you can buy through your employer or your retirement plan. If this option is available to you, it is a good idea to look into it as a way to begin investing. You will be able to invest in mutual funds for free and you will be able to get started quickly and easily with little effort on your part.

What kinds of mutual funds should I look for:

There are many kinds of mutual funds available to choose from. When you begin investing, you may want to start with index funds or a target-date fund. These types of mutual funds invest in many different stocks all at the same time, which can help protect against substantial losses if one company does poorly.

An index fund is a type of mutual fund that buys shares from many different companies that make up a particular segment of the stock market such as technology or healthcare.

A target-date fund buys shares in different companies based on the year that it is set up for (such as 2021) and the date when it expires (such as 2041).

This type of fund allows investors to take advantage of the fact that some companies are doing better than others in different areas in any given year so they don't have to pick individual stocks.

When you begin investing, you are going to need to be patient and you are going to need to be willing to put in the time if you want your investment to grow. You will have a lot of chances to make mistakes or do things that you will regret later on.

This is why you need to talk with someone who has experience investing before you start. You may want to go online and talk with people who are experienced investors or just talk with someone who knows more about investing than you do.

The more information that you can get before your first investment, the better off that you will be in the long run.

For your investment to grow, you need to do more than just buy a mutual fund or stocks and then forget about them. You have to research which companies are doing well when they go public so that when an opportunity comes up, you can take advantage of it.

If this happens, then the chances are good that your money will grow substantially over time as long as the stock market continues on the same path overall.

Should you invest in bonds or mutual funds?

Bonds are issued by corporations, cities, and government agencies. They are created as a way to raise money to be used on projects. The key here is that they are loans that must be repaid at a later date. If you invest in bonds, you may want to choose from those with a fixed rate of interest. Bonds issued by governments or the U.S. Treasury tend to have the lowest rate of interest for an investment of this type.

Bond values tend to move in the opposite direction of interest rates. If interest rates go down, bond prices will rise and vice versa. If you believe that interest rates will fall in the future, then you should buy bonds now before they do go down and suffer from falling bond prices later on when they do fall in value with rising interest rates.

Bond investments have their risks involved with them as well though:

- The issuer may not pay back all of your investment if it can't afford to do so;
- Interest rate changes can also negatively affect the value of your investment; and,
- There is no guarantee that you will receive any return on your investment whatsoever (depending upon what type of bonds it is).

Overall, if you are looking for a safe investment, then bonds may be your best bet.

Should you buy gold or silver?

Some people believe that the best investment for beginners is buying precious metals such as gold and silver. They believe that the value of these metals will continue to increase over time. If you are looking for a safe investment then this is an option you should consider.

What are the advantages of buying gold?

There are several advantages to investing in gold or silver:

- Inflation hedge: The reason why some investors buy gold is that they believe that it will protect them from inflation, especially during periods when there is high inflation. Gold and silver don't tend to respond well to periods of high inflation. This means that if there is a period with high inflation, these precious metals can appreciate. This makes them a very good hedge against inflation and other types of economic stresses such as periods when interest rates are going up fast.
- Inflationary currency: Gold also tends to be a good investment during times when the currency isn't doing well or even if it collapses altogether. This is because investors often use gold to store their wealth during times when their currency isn't safe enough or reliable enough for storage purposes. They will look at places like Switzerland and other European countries where people keep their gold. If the US dollar were to collapse, you would want to have some gold investments as well as having your wealth elsewhere such as in a foreign bank account.
- Protection from market volatility: Another advantage of gold is that it can help protect you against market volatility. It tends to be less volatile than other assets such as stocks and bonds. This makes it an excellent instrument for investors who are looking to protect their portfolios from big losses.

What are the disadvantages of investing in gold?

There are also some things that you need to keep in mind when investing in gold and silver:

- Not liquid: One of the biggest disadvantages of buying and selling precious metals is that they aren't very liquid. This means that it can be very difficult and expensive to buy and sell them at any time. You will need a lot of capital to buy metals like gold and silver because they can be expensive. You may not be able to get them out when you want them if there is a run on the market for these metals or if there is something else going on in the economy that makes them hard to buy or sell quickly at a reasonable price on the open market. The high transaction fees associated with buying and selling precious metals can be expensive. You will need to allocate a substantial amount of your investment capital to buy gold or silver.
- Physical storage: Another disadvantage is that you may be required to store the precious metals physically. This may require you to purchase a safe or some other type of very secure container to hold them in. This can be expensive. It can also be costly if you have to buy insurance for the precious metals that you own.

There are many advantages and disadvantages associated with investing in gold and silver. You must consider all of the pros and cons before making your decision on what type of investment vehicle or strategy you want to use for your portfolio.

Chapter 3: When to start investing?

The best time to start investing is now! Thinking of investing? Whether you've been living on your own for years or you just moved out, this guide is for you.

This chapter will show you why it's never too early to start saving and investing money. You'll also learn the basics about investing, and how to get started. If you're already familiar with some of these things, feel free to skip ahead.

Why should I start investing now?

That's a great question! You've probably heard someone say that the best time to start saving is when you're young, but what does that mean? When do young people have the most financial freedom? What can they do with their extra money that doesn't require much effort?

When you're young you don't make a lot of money yet. But here's the thing: with less income, it means fewer expenses too! That means it's easier for young adults to save and invest because they don't have many expenses yet (like a mortgage or car payments), so they have more money left over at the end of the month.

That's the first thing that makes time your biggest advantage: you have more time to save up. Think about it: if you start saving and investing money when you're young, you'll be able to invest for a longer period and build a bigger nest egg. By investing early, you'll have more time for that money to grow, giving your investments more time for compound growth.

The second thing that makes time your biggest advantage is that the stock market's likely higher when you invest later in life. When the stock market goes up, it means that stocks are getting more expensive (stock prices rise). That means that if you want to buy shares later in life, you'll have to pay more money for them than if you had bought them earlier on. That's why starting early is important: when a person invests $10,000 at 25 years old versus 35 years old, they'd end up with $192,978 at age 65 instead of just $115,958!

Finally, the third thing that makes time your biggest advantage is compound growth! When we talk about "compound growth," we mean how much interest or investment gains earn interest or investment gains themselves. For example...if you invest $100,000 and earn 10% interest, it means that the next year you'll have $110,000. Now, if you earn 10% interest again, you'll have $121,000. Simple steps like that keep adding up over time until you have something huge!

When you invest early in life, you get to use compound growth to your advantage. So yes, investing early is worth it!

There is no "right" time

The reason why you want to invest might be different from someone else. Are you looking to retire early? Do you want to save for a house? Or are you just looking for a way to get started with personal finance?

Whatever your reason, investing is the best way to reach your goals.

The earlier you start, the better:

There are pros and cons of investing when you're young. But most experts agree that young people have an advantage when it comes to investing. Here's why: Your financial time horizon is longer. Your income (from a job or investments) is likely to increase over time. And you have more time to make up for any losses you might experience.

In other words, if you invest when you're young, your money has more time to grow. When you're older, the opposite is true. You'll need to save more money because you won't have as much time to invest.

Let's look at an example of two people, Suzie and Tom: Suzie and Tom both want to buy a house in 5 years. Suzie starts investing in her 20s, while Tom waits until he's 30 years old to start investing. Here's how their investments would compare after 5 years: Suzie invests $5,000 each year for 5 years – a total of $25,000

- Tom starts investing $5,000 each year for 5 years – a total of $25,000
- Both earn 8% interest per year on their investments – a safe average return

After 5 years:

- Suzie has invested $50,000 in total – she has earned $3,944 in interest ($2497.78 + $1747.22)
- Tom has invested $50,000 in total – he has earned $2,944 in interest ($1497.78 + $1747.22)

Suzie is further ahead because she invested more money when she was younger – she had a long time to take advantage of the interest and compound growth.

Tom's investments will start to catch up when he's 45 years old (when Suzie is 35 years old). Suzie will have a larger investment by that time, and the two will be equal when Suzie is 50 years old. Invest at least 10% of your income: The earlier you start investing, the better.

But how much should you invest?

The best answer is "as much as you can". But if you're just getting started with investing, it's not realistic to save 50% or more of your income. That's why we recommend saving at least 10% of your income as a starting point. By saving 10% of your income each year, you'll be able to invest enough to make a difference over time.

How much do you need to save?

To figure out how much money you need to start investing, think about how much you want to save. To make your goal a reality, you'll need to set aside money from each paycheck. One good way to start is by setting up a separate savings account with your bank or credit union. That way, your money is easy to access in case of an emergency. Just make sure you won't be tempted to spend it!

How do I know if I'm saving enough?

If you want to invest for retirement, a good rule of thumb is to save at least 10% of your income every year for retirement. If you're saving for something else, like a house or car, that amount is likely to be higher. Start with 10%, and adjust as needed: If you can't save 10%, that's okay! The important thing is to start saving as soon as you can. Even if you can only save a small amount each month, you're doing better than nothing.

Chapter 4: What are some good tips for investing?

This chapter will give you some tips on how to invest, and what to look for. There are many different ways to invest in the stock market, and you should find what works best for you. You should always do your research before you invest in anything.

These tips are great for anyone, but they are especially good for beginners. There is a lot of information on the internet, and it can be hard to tell what is valuable information and what isn't.

You can learn a lot from the mistakes of others, so this chapter will include some successful investing tips from some of the biggest names in the retail investor markets.

Asset allocation and diversification

Diversification is when you invest in different assets. It is important to diversify because if you invest in too many shares of one company, that can put your investment at risk.

If the company goes bankrupt or has financial problems, you could lose all of your money. If the company does well, however, you could make a significant amount of money.

If you diversify your portfolio (investing in different things), then if one investment goes bad you won't lose everything. You want to spread your investments out so that if one investment fails, it won't cause the other investments to fail as well. This is why beginners need to learn about asset allocation and diversification.

What is asset allocation?

Asset allocation is when you divide up your investments into different categories. For example stocks, bonds, mutual funds, and real estate are all different types of assets that can be included in an asset allocation plan. You can group them by their price range or by how safe they are (risk). An example of a safe group might be bonds and real estate which are considered lower risk options. A group considered risky might be stocks that have a higher chance of losing value.

You should always diversify by including at least some low-risk options, or you could just invest in higher-risk options and lose everything if the stock market goes down. It is up to you what you decide to do, but it is important to be aware of asset allocation and diversification.

What is diversification?

Diversification means that you will have different assets in your portfolio (investment group). You can also include different types of investments within each asset class. If you have a mutual fund that invests in bonds, then it would be considered diversified because it has multiple investments. If all of your investments were stocks, then that would not be considered diversified. The less risky assets should make up more of the portfolio because they are safer and less likely to cause big losses. You should consider adding more riskier assets into your portfolio as well (like stocks) so that you can get a better return on your investment.

Don't get scared by market volatility

If you are a beginner, you may be afraid that your investment will lose all of its value. That is not the case. Many people think that if the market is down it means that their investment is down. This isn't true because when one share of the stock goes down, there is always another share that goes up.

If you have invested wisely and spread out your money in different places, then your investment will not be as volatile as the market. Even if some of your investments go up and some go down, it doesn't mean that you have lost any money at all. All of these investments will still be worth something and you can continue to hold onto them until they get back to their original price.

Since this is probably a major fear for beginners, there are many ways that you can protect yourself from these risks:

First: You can always put some of your money into cash or bonds which will be guaranteed not to lose any value and increase in value over time.

Second: You can diversify your portfolio by investing in different types of companies and industries at different times when prices are low so they're more affordable for new investors like yourself. There are many companies out there that offer different investment plans that are specifically for beginners.

Use the power of compounding

This is one of the biggest tips for investing that you can do. Compounding will allow you to make more money in the stock market by leaving your money in longer.

It works like this: If you put $1,000 into a bank account that is earning 10% interest per year, then in one year it will be worth $1,100. You can leave that money in the bank, and it will get 10% interest again next year so that it would be worth $1,210. You can keep doing this forever, so after 30 years your initial $1,000 could be worth $8226. That's why compounding is such an important part of investing.

Long-term investing is a great idea for beginners because it allows you to leave your money in the market longer. It's good to have a mix of stocks, bonds, and cash in your portfolio. Stocks will give you the highest returns, but they will also be more volatile. Bonds will give you lower returns but they are less volatile.

Cash can be used as a buffer when your investment portfolio loses money during a market downturn. Cash is generally not as good an investment as stocks or bonds, but it is very useful to have some on hand for emergencies or unexpected expenses.

Keep Investing Costs Low

Keeping costs low when investing is very important. Costs are fees that you pay for using certain investment products or services from a broker.

They generally come from two different sources:

Commissions or loads: These are fees that you pay for selling stocks or mutual funds. Commissions can be a flat fee, like $10, or a percentage of your investment, like 1%. You can avoid these fees by using an online broker like Scottrade and investing in low-cost index funds.

Mutual fund expenses: These are the annual fees that you pay to invest in a mutual fund. They usually range from 0.5% to 2%, but some low-cost index funds have expenses under 0.3%. These fees are a bit higher than commissions, but they are still much lower than the fees to invest in actively managed mutual funds.

Keep your costs low by investing in low-cost index funds or ETFs. If you do choose to invest in actively managed mutual funds, then make sure that they have a low expense ratio and do not have any loads. Most actively managed mutual funds will have at least one fund with a low expense ratio.

Don't panic when the market drops

Even the most seasoned investors will tell you that a stock market is a volatile place. It is constantly changing, and it is impossible to know what it will do next.

Although you should always strive to make wise investments, you should also be aware that there will likely be some times when you will lose money. It is not something that can be avoided, but how you handle these losses can make a big difference in the long run.

When a stock drops in value it is called a loss, but this doesn't mean that everything has been lost. The loss on one stock can be offset by the profit from another investment so if you have made wise investments in the past, then your overall portfolio should still be above water.

You might feel like your heart has been ripped out of your chest when the market drops, but try not to panic. This will only lead to poor decisions which can make things worse for you in the long run. You should never invest money based on emotion; instead, focus on making sound financial decisions that benefit your portfolio as a whole.

For example, if you have an investment that has lost a lot of value, you might want to sell it off and move the money to a different investment. However, if the market drops, then the stock could drop even more. You might think that you are saving yourself from further losses by getting rid of this investment, but in reality, you could be making a big mistake.

If your investment is already down by 50%, then it would be foolish to sell it just because it dropped another 10%. If you wait until the stock fully recovers then your overall portfolio will receive a boost which will offset any losses that were sustained during the downturn. It is better to hold on and wait for the market to rebound than it is to let emotions take over and make rash decisions.

The importance of rebalancing your portfolio

One of the best tips for investing is to never buy and hold in the stock market. You should always regularly invest in stocks, or even mutual funds, but you should also regularly sell what you don't want anymore. This strategy is called rebalancing your portfolio.

This means that if a stock or fund is doing well, you might want to invest more of your money into it. However, if a stock or fund isn't doing well, then you might want to sell it and invest that money into something else that is doing better. This will help to maximize your profits as an investor.

This method of investing works particularly well with mutual funds because they allow you to buy a small piece of many different stocks at once. You can then pick and choose what stocks you would like to keep in your portfolio at any given time.

You can also take this approach by only investing in certain sectors of the market for a certain period. For example, if the oil industry is doing well then you might not want to sell off all your oil stocks right away because they are doing well. Instead, you could try buying more shares in companies that are associated with oil so that they will also do well. When the oil industry starts to decline you can then sell off your stocks and use that money to invest in something else.

Take advantage of tax-free savings accounts

When you invest in the stock market, you want to make sure that you're not losing any money. One way to avoid losing money is to use tax-free savings accounts. They are available through the government, and they can help your investments grow faster.

There are many different types of TFSAs that you can choose from, but they all have a few things in common. First of all, your money can't be withdrawn until you reach age 65. Secondly, it's always better to save money every month than to try and save a high amount once a year. You'll have more time for your investments to grow, and more time for your investment account to grow as well.

One of the biggest reasons why people use TFSA accounts is because they're free of tax on growth and income! This means that if your investments go up in value, or if you make a profit from selling stocks or other investments, you won't be taxed for it! Some other accounts that might tax this income include RRSPs or RRIFs - which are also great accounts to use.

If your account grows in value by 35% while it's growing within a TFSA, then when you withdraw the money, you won't be taxed. If your account grows in value by 10% while it's growing within an RRSP, then when you withdraw the money, you will be taxed on these profits.

Many people don't realize how much tax they're paying every year until they start using a TFSA. This is one of the biggest reasons why these accounts are so popular. Use them!

Chapter 5: Investment Ideas

The stock market has been the biggest investment sector in the world which is a backbone for the growth of businesses. It is the definition of wealth and prosperity. For years, it has been known as a way to be successful in life. People have been investing for ages and have seen huge returns on their investments.

It is an ideal way to accumulate money for your future generations or for any other purposes you may have in mind. It is an investment that pays you huge amounts over some time but it takes patience, research, and effort to succeed in this field.

When you are investing, there are several things to consider such as your risk appetite, your age, and other things like return on investment or ROI that should be attractive.

Here are some investment ideas for beginners that are a must to consider.

Growth investing

This section provides an overview of growth investing and why it is the most popular investment strategy. It also explains what growth stocks are and how they can be used to diversify your portfolio.

Growth Stocks

Growth stocks are stocks that have high growth potential. These are the companies that will create a lot of value in the future and have a significant impact on your portfolio. They are identified by their ability to grow earnings faster than the GDP growth rate (5%).

The main difference between growth stocks and value stocks is that growth stocks are expected to grow at above-average rates while value stocks are expected to generate above-average returns from price appreciation (as they trade for less than their intrinsic value).

To identify a good growth stock, you should look for high growth rates, strong balance sheets, high levels of profitability, good management, and brand name. Some investors also prefer to focus on companies with little or no debt (debt-free companies).

Understanding the strategy

Growth investing is a strategy that focuses on companies with strong growth potential. If you want to diversify your portfolio, then you should include growth stocks in your portfolio as they will help you achieve high returns over long periods.

If you are new to investing, then growth stocks are also the best place to start as they will allow you to grow your money quickly. In the long-term, growth stocks can deliver double-digit returns with limited risk.

Growth investing is not suitable for everyone because it involves higher risk than value and defensive investing. It is also very important to understand that when it comes to growth investing, it's not all about the numbers. These companies have to grow at a rate that matches the expectations of their investors. Otherwise, their stock prices will fall significantly and their momentum will disappear (which will be reflected in their share prices).

If you expect a company's earnings growth rate or revenue growth rate to match its market's expectations and demand from investors, then this means that you have a very high return expectation from these companies (which makes them risky). Therefore, only experienced investors should consider using this strategy as it involves higher risk than value and defensive investing (as well as growth investing).

Growth investing works because many investors like to invest in companies that have high growth potential. These are often large and established companies with strong brand names that have been around for many years (such as Microsoft, Google, Coca-Cola, and Walt Disney). As they are growing at fast rates, their stock prices will also be growing at fast rates which means that they will be great investments for long-term focused investors who want to achieve high returns with limited risk over long periods.

The 5% growth rate mentioned above is based on the GDP growth rate which is also the overall growth rate of any economy. It is possible to achieve much higher growth rates than this but it will depend on the size of the company. For example, if a small company grows at a rate above 5% a year, it will offer better returns than a large company with the same growth rate due to its higher risk and smaller market cap.

Diversifying with Growth Stocks

Growth stocks are a great way to diversify your portfolio because they can reduce the risk of your investment. If you want to benefit from the growth potential of a stock, then you should invest in multiple stocks that offer this opportunity. This way, if one company fails to deliver, then you can still benefit from the other companies.

It is also very important to pay attention to the companies that are part of your portfolio because if you invest in stocks that have strong growth potential but do not deliver on it, then your portfolio will suffer. Therefore, it's important to diversify by investing in both growth stocks and value stocks.

How to identify stocks that have the best chance to explode

Growth investing is all about identifying companies with excellent growth potential. This is why growth investors are always on the lookout for stocks that have the best chance to explode. These are their main characteristics:

Strong balance sheet

The company's balance sheet should be in good shape. If there is no or very little debt, then this is even better. Growth companies usually have high levels of profitability and cash flows and therefore, they don't need to borrow money from banks or other lenders. If a company has excessive debt, then it will struggle to grow at a rapid pace because it will have to spend a lot of money on interest payments (this will negatively affect its performance).

Strong management team

If the management team is strong, then the company stands a better chance at growing fast than those with weak management teams. This is because strong management teams have more experience in managing companies and are therefore able to drive the company's growth.

Strong brand name

The brand name is very important when it comes to growth investing. A good brand name increases the company's visibility which makes investors more interested in it. This means that investors will be willing to pay a higher price for this stock, which means that the company will have a lot of funds available to grow at a rapid pace. This is why you should always be on the lookout for companies with strong brands (i.e. Tesla or Apple).

Stocks from which is it better to stay away

There are also stocks that you should stay away from if you want to use a growth investing strategy. These are growth stocks that have very high expectations from their investors, but they don't deliver. Here are a few examples:

Netflix (NFLX) - Netflix is a company with great growth potential, but it has not been able to meet the expectations of its investors. At first, its stock was overvalued and then it became undervalued as the company failed to meet its growth targets. This means that many of its investors lost money with this stock. It's important to note that the company has recovered from this situation and is now trading at a reasonable price, but it still hasn't been able to deliver some of its expectations. As an investor, you should avoid high-risk stocks such as Netflix to minimize your overall risk exposure in your portfolio.

Tesla (TSLA) - Tesla is another example of a high-risk stock because many people expected it to deliver even bigger profits than Ford and General Motors by now (based on the demand for its products and profitability). However, Tesla has been struggling with profitability due to problems in scaling up production. This shows how extreme investor expectations can make a company's stock undervalued or overvalued in the short term.

Growth investing can be a great strategy for investors who want to achieve high returns over the long-term with limited risk exposure. However, you should always focus on quality companies with strong fundamentals and little or no debt. As an investor, it is your responsibility to study companies and avoid high-risk stocks because they will lead you to lose your money over time.

P/E and P/B ratio

The price-to-earnings ratio (or P/E ratio) is the price of a share divided by its earnings per share. P/E ratio is one of the most popular financial ratios because it allows investors to compare the valuation of different companies. The higher the P/E ratio, the more expensive the stock is.

The price to book value (or P/B ratio) is another popular valuation metric. It's calculated by dividing the current market value of a company by its book value (or net asset value). The higher the P/B ratio, the less expensive a stock is.

For example, if a stock has a P/B ratio of 1 (P/B = 1), then it means that the market value of the company is equal to its book value. On the other hand, if a stock has a P/B ratio of 4 (P/B = 4), then it means that the company is worth 4 times more than its book value.

The reason why investors like to compare P/E and P/B ratios when it comes to growth stocks is that they can easily identify companies with high growth potential. In other words, when you compare their price to earnings or price to book values, you automatically know which ones are good investments and which ones are not.

Growth investing can be very rewarding if you choose the right stock, but it can also be very risky if you don't pick the right company. Therefore, before starting your investment process, you should do your research and find out which companies are good investments (based on their current performance and prospects).

Value Investing

Value investing requires a lot of research and analysis. Value investors are very cautious investors. They invest for the long term, not for short-term gains.

Undervalued Stocks

Value investing is a strategy where an investor looks for current market prices that are lower than the intrinsic value of a company. Value investors look at various factors such as current and future growth rate, earnings, cash flow, return on equity, and price to book ratio to find out if the company is undervalued.

Value investing is often confused with "growth investing". Unlike value investors who look for undervalued stocks, growth investors look for stocks with a high potential of growth in terms of earnings.

The best example of value investing is Warren Buffet who has proven that it can be very effective over long periods. In his most recent letter to shareholders, he said: "We have made no changes in our basic investment principles during this period, nor have we deviated from our emphasis on the purchase of equities at attractive prices".

Understanding the strategy

Value investors seek stocks of companies that are selling at a discount from their intrinsic value. When a stock is trading below its true worth, it is said to be undervalued or underpriced. Value investors focus on buying stocks that are not only underpriced but have strong growth potential as well.

The key to being successful in value investing is finding the right balance between fundamental analysis and technical analysis. Fundamental analysis involves studying the financial statements of the company and understanding how it operates compared to competitors in the market but without much focus on its price movements whereas technical analysis involves looking into price movements, analyzing charts, and doing other mathematical calculations without much focus on how a company operates or what its financial statements look like (more to come on technical analysis later).

It is essential to perform your research before making an investment decision because no one can predict market movements 100%. There have been many great books written about value investing and they all have some common themes in them – they all emphasize finding companies that are selling at a discount from their true worth and having strong growth potential.

Identifying stocks

Value investors look for stocks that are undervalued in the market. There are several ways to find out which stocks are undervalued.

An investor can do a fundamental analysis of the stock and then compare the stock with its peers based on various parameters such as price to book ratio, dividend yield, return on equity, etc. The important thing is to find out if the stock is undervalued relative to its peers.

For example, suppose you find a stock that has a price to book ratio of 1 and its peer has a price to book ratio of 8. This means that you have found a company with an intrinsic value of 8 times its current market price. Once you buy this company, if the market realizes that it is overvalued, it will get corrected and could go even lower than it was before making huge profits for you!

The other way is through technical analysis by looking at charts and indicators. A good stock picker who uses both fundamental and technical analysis will be at an advantage since he can use both methods effectively.

Once you have identified stocks that have value potential, there are two ways of investing in those companies:

1. Buy and hold:

This is a very simple method. Just buy the stock and wait for it to appreciate over time. This works great over the long term but you might be waiting for a very long time to see any returns! You might even lose money if a recession hits the market.

2. Buy and sell:

The other way is to buy stocks that are undervalued and sell them when they become overvalued in the market. An investor can do this by using technical analysis based on charts, indicators, etc. This is a risky way of investing because you need to be right at least half the time to make money consistently using this method. If you are wrong too many times, you will end up losing money!

Intrinsic Value

The intrinsic value of a stock is the actual value of a company. This is the value that an investor would have if he purchases the entire company. This can be considered as the theoretical value of a stock.

Value investing does not consider this theoretical value but instead, tries to find stocks that are trading below their intrinsic value in the market.

What is Graham Number?

The Graham Number is used by value investors to find out if a stock is undervalued or not. It was developed by Benjamin Graham, who was also Warren Buffet's mentor at Columbia Business School where he taught him value investing techniques which were later used by Warren Buffet in his investments.

The formula for calculating Graham Number is as follows: Where N = required rate of return (10% or 15%), D = Current earnings (before interest and taxes), and PV = Market value of the company. This number is called the Graham Number.

It is calculated based on the required rate of return. Stocks that are trading below their Graham number are considered to be undervalued. To make it easier, most investors say that if the Graham Number is less than 20, then it is undervalued.

Graham Number can also be used to calculate a stock's intrinsic value using discounted cash flow method.

In this formula, you use a 10% discount rate to calculate the present value of future cash flows using the Graham formula: Where P0 = Current stock price, CF0 = Cash flow in t0 year, r = required rate of return and t = number of years for cash flow.

If you use this formula to find out if your stock has a margin of safety or not, you will get an exact number for Graham Number which can be compared with the current price to see if it is overvalued or not by comparing the current price with discounted cash flow method (Graham Number).

It should be noted that this approach uses the DCF method while calculating a stocks' intrinsic value so it might not be reliable since its assumptions may not hold in reality; they are often tweaked to make the numbers work out.

Income Investing

There are different types of income investments. The most common type of income investing is bonds, preferred stocks, and government-issued bonds.

Income investing is the process of generating income from your investments. Income investing is different from capital investment, which is expected to generate returns in the form of capital gains.

Understanding the strategy

Income investing is about getting a steady and consistent stream of income from your investment portfolio. You can expect to receive this income regardless of the performance of the market.

This makes it ideal for the conservative investor who wants to protect their portfolio from dips in the market without having to sacrifice a consistent source of stream income.

With bonds, preferred stocks, and government-issued bonds you can expect an interest payment every six months or annual interest payments if you invest in Treasury Bonds. The interest rate will vary from bond to bond but you can typically expect a return between 3% and 7%.

With preferred stocks, the period you will receive a dividend payment once per year or quarterly if you invest in preferred stocks that pay a monthly dividend. The dividend payments can be anywhere between 2% and 10% per year depending on how many shares you own and the type of stock itself.

These are just examples and there are plenty more types of income investments that we will cover soon!

Dividend-paying stocks

Dividend stocks are stocks that pay out dividends. To identify dividend-paying stocks, you can look at the company's financial statements. Each company's financial statement has an income statement that gives details of the company's revenues and expenses.

The company will have a list of its dividends paid. Dividends are typically paid quarterly, and investors expect to see a high yield from dividend-paying stocks.

Bonds

Bonds are debt instruments issued by governments or companies to fund their ongoing operations or to fund projects like building a new plant or buying machinery for their operations. Bonds may be issued in any currency but are most commonly issued in US dollars (US-denominated) and British pounds (GBP-denominated).

The interest rate on a bond is fixed at the time of the issue by the issuing entity, which is usually a government or corporation. This means that you know how much interest you will receive every year until the bond expires.

The bond pays interest for a fixed period of time, after which it matures, meaning it becomes due and payable then. When you buy an income bond, you agree with the issuing entity to pay back its principal amount on the maturity date and, also, receive interest payments every year.

Bonds may be purchased through a broker. The issuing entity will offer you a choice of bonds to buy, each with different interest rates. You can choose the one that best meets your investment objectives. You can also compare bond prices offered by different brokers to get the best price for the bond with the characteristics you want.

ETFs and mutual funds

ETF (Exchange-traded fund) is a type of fund that owns assets, such as stocks and bonds. It trades on an exchange just like the stock. Mutual funds are pools of money that are owned by the investors in the mutual fund. Mutual funds are managed by a professional investment manager.

An ETF is traded during its day trading session, while a mutual fund is bought or sold only at the end of its trading day. An ETF has a management fee, while a mutual fund does not have any management fees.

An ETF owns the stocks it tracks, while mutual funds do not own their assets. Mutual funds have their net asset value calculated daily at 4 pm, while an ETF's net asset value is available only at the close of the trading day.

An ETF trades like a stock, while a mutual fund cannot be traded in fractions as you can with an ETF. You can buy an ETF directly from its issuer, while you need to buy a mutual fund through your broker or agent.

Preferred Stocks

Preferred stocks are hybrid investments that give you some characteristics of both stocks and bonds. Like bonds, preferred stocks offer fixed dividend payments every year.

The dividend rate is typically higher than the dividend paid by common stocks. Like common stocks, preferred stocks are traded on an exchange and have no maturity date.

Preferred stocks are issued by corporations and governments, just like bonds and common stocks. To buy preferred stocks, you need to establish an account with a broker who trades in this type of security.

The broker will provide you details of the preferred stock on offer and let you know how much it costs to purchase a share of that security.

Once again, it is important to compare prices offered by different brokers to get the best price for the preferred stock with the characteristics you want.

Indexing

In general, index funds are a good place to start because they are relatively simple. You simply buy the entire market and let it run for a while. Keep in mind that your returns will not be as high as an actively managed fund, but you can do just fine with index funds.

What is an Index Fund?

An index fund is a mutual fund that tracks an index. An index is a computer-generated collection of stocks that are considered to be the best investments in the market.

The two most popular indices are the Dow Jones Industrial Average (or DJIA) and the S&P 500. The Dow Jones Industrial Average consists of 30 large companies and is very good for diversification.

The S&P 500 includes 500 of the largest companies and tends to have more growth potential. Both indices include stocks from all industries and are good for starting portfolios.

You can buy an index fund by using any discount brokerage firm such as Merrill Lynch, E*Trade, Ameritrade, or Charles Schwab.

You can also invest in an index fund at your local bank or credit union if they offer them. They will charge you less than 1% per year unless you have a large account with them, which will usually not be worth it for beginners looking to invest $5000 or less per year unless they invest regularly throughout the year.

If you have larger amounts to invest, then it might be worth going to your local bank or credit union because they will likely charge less than 1% but will still provide you with great service.

Understanding the strategy

Index funds are very easy. You simply buy the entire index. For example, if you invest in an S&P 500 index fund, you buy the entire S&P 500. This ensures that you own all 500 stocks in the S&P 500.

There is no need to pick and choose which stocks to invest in because the computer does it for you. You also don't need to worry about whether or not a manager is doing a good job of managing funds or not because the computer does it for you.

You can also invest in the Dow Jones Industrial Average which consists of 30 large companies that are considered to be some of the best investments in the market.

These companies include things like Exxon Mobil (XOM), General Electric (GE), Wal Mart Stores (WMT), Johnson & Johnson (JNJ), and many others that are good investments for beginners who don't have a lot of money to invest.

Once an index fund has been created, it will be maintained by a computer program that will buy and sell stocks as they rise and fall in value according to how well they are performing compared to each other or compared to their peers, etc.

Once an investor buys into this index fund, he can then sit back and let the computer do all of the hard work for him.

How to choose the right index fund

Look at the investment minimums

Some funds require you to invest $10,000 or more. If you don't have that kind of money, you can't use that fund. Look for something that has a lower minimum like $500.

Look at the expense ratios

This is important because some index funds have high expense ratios. That means they take a percentage of your investment every year. To find out the expense ratio of a fund, just go to Morningstar or Yahoo Finance and punch in the ticker symbol for that fund and it'll tell you what the expense ratio is like.

So now we know that we want an index fund with a low fee ratio and a low minimum investment amount!

Decide what kind of index you want to invest in

Are you going to invest in US stocks only or are you going to spread your money out amongst multiple markets?

There are many different kinds of indexes, but this isn't an article on how to choose the right one. It's just an example for beginners who don't know how to choose indexes yet. So let's say that we're going with US-only stocks because it's easy.

Then you can go to Morningstar or Yahoo Finance and plug in the ticker symbol for the fund that you want to invest in. You'll find out that there are a bunch of different funds with a similar name. For example, there's Vanguard Total Stock Market Index Fund (VTSMX) and Vanguard Total Stock Market Index Fund Admiral Shares (VTSAX). But these aren't the only two options out there.

There are many other Vanguard index funds, or someones from Schwab, Fidelity, State Street, etc... just plug in the ticker symbol and look at all of your options!

The best thing to do is to read the articles on those funds at Morningstar or Yahoo Finance to see what kind of returns they have been giving lately.

Generally speaking, any fund with good returns will be doing well. But if you have no idea what you're looking at, then stick with one of the top three: Vanguard, Fidelity, or Schwab. They're pretty much always among the best on their respective lists.

Diversify Your Portfolio

Now that you know what index fund(s) you want to invest in, it's time to decide how much you want to invest in each of them.

Should you put 30% in VTSMX and 10% in VTSAX? What about 20% and 5%? How much should you diversify your portfolio?

The answer: enough to make you feel comfortable. Let's say that you have $10,000 saved up. That's a good amount of money to invest so let's go with that. If you were going to invest all of your money into one fund, then you'd want to do something like 75/25 or 60/40 (75% US stocks and 25% international stocks).

But you're not going to do that because it's unwise. So what will it be? 50/50? 25/75? There isn't an exact formula for how much percentage should go into each fund, but there is a general rule that I follow: if one index has a higher return than another, then I will put more money into the higher returning index fund until the returns are about the same.

So if we look at VTSMX and VTSAX, they both have pretty good returns over the last year or two (VTSMX is around 10% while VTSAX is around 8%), so we'll put 50% of our money into VTSMX and the other 50% in VTSAX.

I'm not going to go over how to go about investing because there are several different ways that you can do it.

Conclusion

We have come to the end of our Beginners' Guide to Investing. There is so much more that can be said on this subject, but we have tried to keep this guide short and simple. There are many great books out there that can give you more in-depth information on the topics we have talked about.

You should be able to start implementing some of the techniques and ideas we have talked about into your investment plan. Remember that investing in a diversified portfolio of different types of assets is key to preventing substantial losses in the event a stock or asset class declines in value.

It is important to remember that everyone's situation is different and there are no guarantees in the market. To be successful, you need to fully understand the risks involved and do your research before investing.

We hope this guide has been helpful for you! Good luck!

www.ingramcontent.com/pod-product-compliance
Lightning Source LLC
Chambersburg PA
CBHW071112220526
45467CB00004B/1823